Little Laureates

Edited By Byron Tobolik

First published in Great Britain in 2021 by:

Young Writers
Remus House
Coltsfoot Drive
Peterborough
PE2 9BF
Telephone: 01733 890066
Website: www.youngwriters.co.uk

All Rights Reserved
Book Design by Ashley Janson
© Copyright Contributors 2020
Softback ISBN 978-1-80015-198-7

Printed and bound in the UK by BookPrintingUK
Website: www.bookprintinguk.com
YB0457E

★ FOREWORD ★

Welcome Reader!

Are you ready to discover weird and wonderful creatures that you'd never even dreamed of?

For Young Writers' latest competition we asked primary school pupils to create a Peculiar Pet of their own invention, and then write a poem about it! They rose to the challenge magnificently and the result is this fantastic collection full of creepy critters and amazing animals!

Here at Young Writers our aim is to encourage creativity in children and to inspire a love of the written word, so it's great to get such an amazing response, with some absolutely fantastic poems. Not only have these young authors created imaginative and inventive animals, they've also crafted wonderful poems to showcase their creations and their writing ability. These poems are brimming with inspiration. The slimiest slitherers, the creepiest crawlers and furriest friends are all brought to life in these pages – you can decide for yourself which ones you'd like as a pet!

I'd like to congratulate all the young authors in this anthology, I hope this inspires them to continue with their creative writing.

★ CONTENTS ★

Balbeggie Primary School, Balbeggie

Eva Malloch (10)	1
Summer Gourlay (10)	2
Topaz Petrie (10)	3
Caoimhe Simpson (11)	4
Aiden Sharples (11)	5
Emily Manson (9)	6
Zoey Kareen Kelly (10)	7
Billy Lunn (9)	8
Danielle Barrie (9)	9
Theo Appleyard (8)	10
Harvey Swan (9)	11
Jamie Turpie (10)	12
Eoin Philip (9)	13

Didsbury CE Primary School, Didsbury

Emma Meredith (9)	14
Ben Wheatley (7)	15
Anna Donnelly (7)	16
Caitlin Arundale (10)	17
George Reeve (7)	18
Noel Day (7)	19
Hugh Meredith (7)	20

Horsenden Primary School, Greenford

Lisa Jammeh (10)	21
Laila Noor Hussain (10)	22
Hayden Howells (10)	24
Caleb Macdonald-Petterson (9)	25
Rudra Patel (10)	26

Zidane Benamar (9)	28
Mateusz Trzcinski (9)	29
Stella Campbell-White (9)	30
Dhruvi Gohil (9)	31
Tiara Maqedonci (9)	32
Afnan Hossain (11)	33
Emil Rozak (9)	34
Jakub Konwent (9)	35
Radhika Bhesania (9)	36
Sharu Vijayaramanan (9)	37
Sarah Obikpe (9)	38
Aranie Thasan (9)	39
Adam Wisowaty (10)	40
Jana Alhrouk (10)	41
Cyrus Parangi (9)	42
Julia Bielecka (9)	43
Nadia Przybyszewska (11)	44
David Ogiela (10)	45
Niti Upadhyay (11)	46
Faye Mushatat (10)	47
Aarav Shah (10)	48
Vibishan Kamalahasan (10)	49
Atiya Stachowiak (10)	50
Maria Danilczyk (10)	51
Lucy-Sophie Gharapetian (10)	52
Ahmed Muhday (10)	53
Yasmine Mrimou-Cahill (11)	54
Aaliya Bhachu (10)	55
Thayan Meisuria (9)	56
Hibba Ashraf (10)	57
Ezzah Maqsood (9)	58
Eryk Ficek (10)	59
Natalie Malwic (10)	60
Julia Zamorska (9)	61
Igor Szewczyk (9)	62

Aria-Niaya Varsani (9)	63
Jan Worytkiewicz (9)	64
Ali Abdul-Saheb (9)	65
Jakub Lawniczak (9)	66
Ruqayyah Alowdany (10)	67

Ludgvan Community Primary School, Ludgvan

Rory Ranson (10)	68
Kyla Curnow (10)	69
Poppy Jacobs (9)	70
Sofia Collins (10)	71
Abby Long (9)	72
Emily Basher (10)	73
Gracie Dyer (9)	74
Alfie Healey (9)	75
Margo Dumbleton (9)	76
Riley Le Seelleur (10)	77
Luke Scott (9)	78
Jessica Townson (9)	79

Simms Cross Primary School, Widnes

Lilly Ella Jerram (9)	80
Salim Ghounay (11)	82
Neave Edwards (10)	84
Bobby Dunning (10)	86
Ava Grace Gatcliffe (10)	87
Spencer Smith-Underwood (10)	88
Miley Fowler (10)	90
Pippa Nelly Magee (10)	92
Emily B (10)	93
Alivia Riley (10)	94
Nicola Palyz (11)	96
Frank Bussey (10)	97
Zeynur Yuseinova (10)	98
Jessica-Lea Downey (9)	99
Lily-Mai Graham-Brown (10)	100
Zen Edison Stokes (9)	101
Eleanor Forshaw (10)	102
Faith Pitt (10)	103
Archie Smith Underwood (10)	104

Jayden Robinson (9)	105
Alfie Rowlands (10)	106
Harry Sheehan (10)	107
Alexi O'Brien	108
Arnas Petrauskas (10)	109
Emily Watson (10)	110
Libby Savage (10)	111
Kelsey Willcox (10)	112
Abigail Atherton (11)	113
Maisie Johns (9)	114
Grace Fowler (10)	115
Joel Machell-McCann (9)	116
Jay Jay Rodgers (10)	117
Patrick McMahon (9)	118
Megan Willcox-Collington (9), Maisy Owens (9), Patrick, Harry Tiernan (9) & Robert Bowen (9)	119
Logan Dunn (10)	120
Kaitlin Dolman (9)	121
Leon Walton (10)	122
Phoebe Batty (9)	123
Alana-Louise (10)	124
Jamie King (10)	125

St Paul's Catholic Primary School, Cheshunt

Leah Overett (9)	126
Georgia Cannell (10)	127
Madison Pell (10)	128
Damian Chudy (10)	129
Laura Rice (9)	130
Tiara Oke (9)	131
Noel Ranasinghe (10)	132
Ava Rose Guy (9)	133
Daniel Marinov (10)	134
Kayra Saffet (11)	135
Ruairí Hickey (10)	136
Valentina Kasa (9)	137
Louie Wallis (10)	138
Joanne Onyearugbulem (9)	139
Chloe Sritharan (10)	140
Honor Hart (9)	141
Leo Alfano (10)	142

Amelia Sobejko (10)	143
Lennon Connolly (10)	144
Cayden Desouza-Singh (9)	145
Ailbe Coleman (10)	146
Isabella Clack (9)	147
Jordan Mutsau (9)	148
Sophia Beckford (10)	149
Mia Frangione (10)	150
Dominika Guszpit (10)	151
Tanus Van Molendorff (9)	152
Maisie Popely (10)	153
Lottie Leake (10)	154
Evie Toms (10)	155
Francesca Smith (10)	156
Millie O'Sullivan (9)	157
Imogen Popely (9)	158
Lorenzo Guglielmucci (11)	159
Ana-Rose Ranasinghe (11)	160
Brady Pell (9)	161
Jalika Jaiteh (11)	162
Isabelle Aliberti (10)	163
Samuel Robson (9)	164
Ryan Gibson (9)	165
Scarlett-Rose Thorogood (9)	166
Nikolai Paton (9)	167
Poppy Saunders (10)	168
Ben Hunger (9)	169
Cally de Silva (10)	170
Isabelle Palmer (9)	171
Israel Teniola (9)	172

Whitehouse Primary School, Elm Tree

Ava Henry (9)	173
Olivia Morrison (9)	174
Daniel Wilson (9)	175
Scarlett Lowe (10)	176
Stanley McDougall (10)	177
Lincoln Turner (10)	178
Alyssia Whalsh (9)	179
Rubin Vallily (9)	180
Jack Devine (9)	181
Katie Kingston (9)	182

Rhys Pink (9)	183
Christine Petrik (9)	184
Guy Honeyman (9)	185
Finlay Tombling (9)	186
Mo Khalid (9)	187
Aleah McGarvey (9)	188
Chyna-Rose Whitton (9)	189
Daiton Lewis (9)	190

THE POEMS

Bonnie The Fashionista

Bonnie is a lovable dog,
She rocks day and night,
In her pink dresses,
Black caps, blue hoodies and more,
She is a dog that all people adore!
Her dream is to be on the front cover of the newest fashion book,
Now let me tell you how her dream came true!
Usually I would make her outfits and she would wear them,
Bonnie is a popular dog, all the dogs know her.
No dog would dare to try take her place,
Or they might get a scratch in the face,
Every Saturday was a photoshoot, but this one was special,
Bonnie had decided to go in 80s retro,
Small glasses, flashy colours, cool caps and more.
When the producer saw Bonnie, he loved her straight away.
Poof! She was on the front cover!
And that's how her dream came true.

Eva Malloch (10)
Balbeggie Primary School, Balbeggie

Benjy: Animal Of The Jungle

Benjy the wolf giraffe,
He has long legs, but a small body.
All his friends laugh and stare,
Nobody dares to go near.
He walks alone in complete silence,
You can't hear a mouse squeak or a bird chirp.
In the night he says a poem:
Why, oh why, must no one like me,
I'm just Benjy, Benjy the wolf giraffe,
I might not look normal,
But I'm still an animal like all of them,
Why can't they see, I'm just Benjy...?
Claps! Benjy gasps in shock,
He turns around to see...
Hedgehog, bird, giraffe, wolf and elephant cheering at him.
He then became the animal of the jungle.

Summer Gourlay (10)
Balbeggie Primary School, Balbeggie

Milo Is A Very Lazy Pen Dog

Any dog can be different,
But not this one.
It can fly, it can dance,
Yes, this dog is amazing.
Little puppy is so good,
Like a superhero.
A dog and a penguin,
At the same time, wow!
Rolling down a mountain, amazing.
Milo is very smelly and lazy too,
He is very annoying because he only likes food,
"Lol!" he says in dog language,
Only likes you for food,
So don't give him food when you feel like it.
Laziest dog in the whole wide world.
A sleepy dog, zzz,
He snores,
You already know what else.

Topaz Petrie (10)
Balbeggie Primary School, Balbeggie

Baboon On The Moon!

I have a lovely pet baboon
Her name is Bertha
Did I mention she can fly?
She also loves pie!
I love my baboon
But enough of that
This is about our trip to the moon!
We put on our helmets
Had some red velvets
And then I got on his back
And there I sat
Until we got to our destination
The stars shone so bright
And that wasn't my imagination!
Bertha hopped and jumped on the moon
What a silly baboon!
We came back down in a cluster
And when we got home
We had our favourite dessert, custard!

Caoimhe Simpson (11)
Balbeggie Primary School, Balbeggie

Toffee The Chef

Toffee the guinea pig loves to cook,
He uses his book,
Toffee loves to make banoffee,
He also loves to make his special cakes,
He cleans his dishes, but he wishes not to,
But today he had a full house,
He had to make something good,
He started to bake his cakes,
He got the sugar cougar and drove to the store,
He got the flour from the tower,
He got his secret sauce,
That he caught flying through the air,
He made the dinner, it was a success,
He was the winner,
He needed to sleep to keep today's memories.

Aiden Sharples (11)
Balbeggie Primary School, Balbeggie

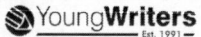

Hejjog

H ejjog is a hog, he has a hedge, so that would make him a hedgehog
E very day he wears his vest because he thinks he is the best
J umping and running every day, but when he is done, he is tired because he has to carry his hedge all the way
J ust listen, did I mention that he is Spanish and has a moustache?
O ver there is his favourite bear, his name is Chair and he is a bear
G et a hog and give it a hedge because hogs with hedges can do a lot of things like go and flush the loo.

Emily Manson (9)
Balbeggie Primary School, Balbeggie

That Little Muffin

This poem is about me and my hamster's trip to the circus

She put on a leotard,
She hopped on my back whilst everybody clapped,
Let's stop talking about clapping and get onto dancing.
She shakes her hips with rakes on her fingertips,
Muffin, the bravest one of all, I'm not even joking,
My favourite experience with her,
Was when she got her updated house,
She went head-first from top floor to bottom floor.
P.S. She's a Gryffindor.

Zoey Kareen Kelly (10)
Balbeggie Primary School, Balbeggie

My Marvellous Snake-Cat!

My marvellous snake-cat is so extraordinary,
It may look ferocious,
But it is quite the opposite and lazy,
But it can go crazy,
My snake-cat is incredible.

My marvellous snake-cat is so extraordinary,
With its light green scales,
And its gigantic furry paws and claws,
It is so marvellous,
My snake-cat is incredible,
It's one of a kind.

Billy Lunn (9)
Balbeggie Primary School, Balbeggie

Pensky

P ensky is a horse/calf, she likes to gallop and slaver
E very day she wears her coat
N ight and day with horses and calves on it
S he rolls and tumbles and runs and jumps
K ind, but when Mel the dog comes, she goes bonkers
Y ou know this animal now, she is kind, friendly, a wee bit bonkers, but very lovable and lots of fun.

Danielle Barrie (9)
Balbeggie Primary School, Balbeggie

Treat

Pets are so weird if you ask me,
Especially my turtle Curdary,
For my turtle, you see him clapping every time,
Little know he is massive for a turtle,
I know I can't find him,
And he is always hiding or clapping,
Ridiculous I know,
Now you know how I feel.

Theo Appleyard (8)
Balbeggie Primary School, Balbeggie

My Dog, Charly

C aring for family
H yper dog
A thletic dog
R unning dog
L iving a life in doggy Heaven
I wish for a good time for her
E xcited to get the new puppy for Christmas, but... I wish you were there to see

Harvey Swan (9)
Balbeggie Primary School, Balbeggie

A Cat Or Two

A cat or two
Biting, scratching, annoying and scared
But so lovely
Meows both cute and excited
Snuggling lazily in the sun
And only goes out when it's dark
She runs away but she is still my cat-panion!

Jamie Turpie (10)
Balbeggie Primary School, Balbeggie

Lana

Dog,
So fluffy and beautiful
Great at finding bones and staring at doors,
Oh so patiently staring at the door.
Waiting and wanting, just hoping she can once again run and be free
My dog, RIP.

Eoin Philip (9)
Balbeggie Primary School, Balbeggie

Blob Dog

It may be a bit lazy and a bit dazy,
But by day its hands turn purple,
And his ears turn purple,
Its belly button will only turn bright red,
Its face goes blue, but not the colour of glue,
On Thursday, Blob Dog might call it 'Fursday',
And on a different day every week,
It will grow two times taller than normal,
It may be odd, it may look weird,
It may be twice the size of a St Bernard's beard,
But I like all dogs,
Even if they look like logs.

Emma Meredith (9)
Didsbury CE Primary School, Didsbury

Stupid Dave

There once was a cat called Dave
He was crazy 'cos he wanted to shave
He jumped in some bins
And his friend made him some din-dins
And boy, they reeked!
He tried picking his nose
But got ink on his clothes
So never tried picking again
Plus, Dave owned a smelly, old fleece
Which attracted a flock of geese
He broke all of the rules
And it angered the school
Whilst Dave was having a lolly.

Ben Wheatley (7)
Didsbury CE Primary School, Didsbury

Hummingbird

Hummingbirds are cute and kind,
They flap their wings 80 times.
When you look upon the sky,
You see they're all up high.
Hummingbirds get very hungry,
That's why they're very grumpy.
In the flowers, you will see down and down,
Deep and deep nectar is there waiting for you,
Would you like to have some too?
Fly, fly, fly away,
Go and find a way to stay.

Anna Donnelly (7)
Didsbury CE Primary School, Didsbury

Unicorn, Cat And Dog

Unicorn is very, very funny,
She loves gloves and doves,
Unicorn is cool, she loves the pool.

Cat can see yellow hollows and follows,
She can smell from a mile,
Cat can feel the air in her hair and feel a bear.

Dog has arms like a bird,
She has a tail as colourful and wonderful as a whale,
Her main body is like newspaper and capers.

Caitlin Arundale (10)
Didsbury CE Primary School, Didsbury

The Very Fat Dog

The very fat dog
He lives in the bog
Once there was a time
Where he was covered in slime
And he slipped and tripped till he died
And became a zombie, but he never tried!
Now he's a zombie,
They don't call him Fat Dog,
They call him Fat Dog Zombie!
Fat Dog Zombie is very stupid
And he doesn't know how to spell his own name!

George Reeve (7)
Didsbury CE Primary School, Didsbury

The Colourful Fish Of Days!

The colourful fish of days
Have a giant craze!
About one tiny fish
That ate a human dish!
Once one of them flew,
And then he died!
Now they can travel through time
But some people call it a crime!
These fish have a disguise
If you see them, you'll be lucky,
But the luckiest is Bucky,
Don't even try, goodbye!

Noel Day (7)
Didsbury CE Primary School, Didsbury

Jeff The Cool Cat!

Jeff the cool cat, he is quite fat!
He never ever kills a rat!
Here he comes with his big tum,
He is really, really fun!
Be careful when you stroke,
Because you'll end up being broke!
Although he looks cute,
He is a bit of a brute!
Please, please do not cry,
There's one word to say,
Goodbye!

Hugh Meredith (7)
Didsbury CE Primary School, Didsbury

Sneaky Snake

Blending in with the pitch-black night,
Nobody can see him, he's out of your sight.
Creeping through the dark, still as a statue
It's horrific when he's already found you

Body like a ruler with a costume unlit
Petrifying stare enough to make anyone quit
Glaring into enemies' souls without a blink
With starless eyes, the colour of ink

There's Raffish Rhino with his horns like knives,
Defeating him, saving everyone's lives.
Bad Baboon swinging tree to tree
He's a coward willing to run and flee

Smooth fur like a baby's cheeks
Guileful Ginger, his sidekick to seek
Serrated swords that love to injure
He saves the world as he's a ninja.

Lisa Jammeh (10)
Horsenden Primary School, Greenford

Shark Head

It all started with my friend Bob,
He was attacked by an angry mob.

When he came back to mine for tea,
I couldn't see his face!

In its place was a sack,
He said, "Help me, all I can see is black!"

I pulled and I tugged very hard,
But when it came off, there was a box
Made out of card,
Covering his face.

We pulled it off and my gasp of astonishment
crescendoed around the room.

Instead of a face...
In that very place...
Was a shark's head!

We called his mum,
She said, "Oh, my dear son!"

She sent him to live in the ocean,
Every day he is fed a potion.

To try and restore him to my old pal Bob,
Who was attacked by an angry mob.

Laila Noor Hussain (10)
Horsenden Primary School, Greenford

Fred, The Pet That Looks Like A Tree

My name is Fred and I've got a very big head,
I've got two faces; one happy, one sad,
It's very handy you see,
As I've also got a body that looks like a tree,
Which is not good when a dog needs a pee!
Some people find me scary,
As my legs are very hairy,
But I'm actually very nice, especially to mice,
They like to visit me,
I can cheer you up with my happy face,
And shake my leaves and jump up and down,
With my hairy legs and knobbly, wobbly knees,
I'm a very different pet that lives outside,
So next time you go for a ride,
Stop, look very closely at the trees,
As you might find a knobbly knee.

Hayden Howells (10)
Horsenden Primary School, Greenford

Litsten

This is a poem about my little Litsten,
Whose monobrow is sometimes blitzin',
He's red and small, but really, really tall,
And he can never crawl,
But can do a handstand to all,
His whiskers are like moles,
If you touch them, people will turn into trolls,
Also, he has six eyes,
Did I mention he likes pies?
He has fins all over his body,
But he can't even swim in a little pondy,
He has six arms, two on his head,
Imagine what happens when he goes to bed,
That was my poem, one and all,
If you don't like it, you are very much cruel.

Caleb Macdonald-Petterson (9)
Horsenden Primary School, Greenford

My Fish That Can Kiss

We know that fish can't fly
And they are very shy

But I have one which does fly
And is not at all shy

When I'm worried
And get my head buried

I look at the tank
And it flies with a yank

When she blinks
I think she winks
When I watch her from the side

When I am happy
I spend time with my guppy

When I am busy
It shines and makes me dizzy

I feed her flakes
And she enjoys them like cakes

When I call her a silly fish
She sends me a flying kiss
And that's something I don't want to miss.

Rudra Patel (10)
Horsenden Primary School, Greenford

Smack: The Perfect Hamster

Smack, he loves to rap,
Everyone calls him a rat,
And he doesn't like that.
He has paws, he has tiny claws,
And he just loves to roar!
He leaps, he yeets,
And cheats in races!
His sunglasses shine when he defeats crime,
And all is now greatly fine.
He smells like Brie cheese,
He likes to eat peas,
And trust me, he's got some speed.
He's got imagination,
He has lots of determination,
And got good relations with the cops.
All he dreams is to be free,
And climb the most tallest tree...

Zidane Benamar (9)
Horsenden Primary School, Greenford

Dream Of A Dog

D ay like normal, maybe not
R unning, running, I will see you soon and I can spend
E xtraordinary day with my friend
A mazing, adorable adventure waiting for us
M arvellous moment when I meet my dog

O ur bodies touch when I stroke you
F luffy, furry, soft, you are so cute

A lways dreaming about you

D oggy, doggy, where are you?
O h, I can feel your slimy tongue on my face
G ood dreams, I hope that my wish will come true.

Mateusz Trzcinski (9)
Horsenden Primary School, Greenford

Penelope The Peculiar Pet Python

- **P** enelope the peculiar pet python prefers painting to pottery and petals to pens
- **Y** ou're soon to see her slipping and sliding in her gross, green garden
- **T** he problem with Penelope the pet python is that she is always hungry
- **H** er favourite food is stinky, smelly, stale steak
- **O** n sunny Sundays, Penelope might share a crumb of her stinky, stale, slimy steak
- **N** asty, naughty Nick is Penelope's best friend and he always shares his slimy, smelly, stale steak with Penelope the pet python.

Stella Campbell-White (9)
Horsenden Primary School, Greenford

Harry The Hamster

Happy, adorable, sassy, wild hamster Harry,
Its fur is soft like a tiger,
It moves like a gigantic truck,
Its dangerous, tiny eyes are brown like chocolate buttons,
Its body is like a colourful oval and slimy,
Its ears are round like a circle and feathery,
Its legs are skinny like a stick with claws,
Its face is like a grumpy pig with scales,
It sounds like a wild mouse with a ferocious smile,
Harry the hamster is still the best, most extraordinary friend and family member too.

Dhruvi Gohil (9)
Horsenden Primary School, Greenford

What Is This I See?

It swims with the ocean breeze,
Its beauty shines throughout the open sea.
Though this beauty may not be seen,
The real beauty is the one you do not see.

I look out to the horizon,
A shadowy figure in sight.
It leaps into the sunset,
Into the free sea...
I don't know what I see,
Are you real or a fantasy?

Just by dawn,
My mind showered with thoughts.
My eyes shut tight,
Lost in my visions.
I wonder,
What is this I see...?

Tiara Maqedonci (9)
Horsenden Primary School, Greenford

Pearl And Posey

I took my pets on a marvellous walk,
With them slithering along the colourful streets,
I fed them colourful treats,
Tail and tentacles wriggling everywhere,
While we walked in the park,
Hissing every now and then,
We met adorable pets and became friends,
Playing catch and football too,
Until it started to rain fresh dew,
So we said goodbye to all our new friends,
Pearl and Posey,
Extraordinary and agile,
Head home at last,
Waiting for another walk.

Afnan Hossain (11)
Horsenden Primary School, Greenford

Super Mog

Every single dog
likes to run in the fog.
Likes to sit on the rock
and look at the playing frog.
My superhero dog
is called Super Mog.
Mog likes to fly
as high as the sky.
He always wears a superhero outfit
but he isn't very fit.
He likes to eat a lot of meat.
Sometimes I want to fly with Mog
when I see him in the fog.
He is the best friend I've ever seen
I can always count on him.

Emil Rozak (9)
Horsenden Primary School, Greenford

Shadowy And His Big Adventure

Shadowy went outside,
He found a building site.

Shadowy loved dragon fruit,
But he heard someone shoot.

When he flew towards the strange building site,
Because he wondered why the light was so bright.

There was a homeless man,
So Shadowy decided to call his friend, Batman.

Now they can save the world together,
Suddenly, there was sunny weather.

Jakub Konwent (9)
Horsenden Primary School, Greenford

Mr Teddy

My dog is called Teddy as he is so fluffy,
Teddy wakes up early to make friends with puppies.
Looking adorable like a model,
He waits for a cuddle.
If something goes wrong,
He growls and barks until it's dark.
Like a human, he crawls on my bed,
And stretches his legs.
When he is cold, he puts on a blanky,
So when he does all those things,
I call him Mr Teddy.

Radhika Bhesania (9)
Horsenden Primary School, Greenford

Dog's Love To Its Owner

You feed me when I'm hungry,
You keep water in my dish,
You let me sleep on anything,
Or in any place I wish.

You sometimes let me lick your hand,
Or even your face,
Despite that, I even licked myself,
In every private place.

You always have my loyalty,
Up to the bitter end,
'Cause now it's plain to see,
You're my best friend.

Sharu Vijayaramanan (9)
Horsenden Primary School, Greenford

My Rainbow Life: My Story!

R espectful to others
A dorable and colourful
I n a happy world
N ice and helpful
B eautiful and smiling
O n the go to help
W onder dog makes everyone happy

D isagreeing to the wrong things
A ble to make people laugh
S o happy, never sad
H elping and caring for others.

Sarah Obikpe (9)
Horsenden Primary School, Greenford

Coco

This is a poem about my peculiar pet,
He is the very best,
Coco is his name,
He loves to play games,
Coco is cute, clever and crazy,
He is funny and friendly,
And loves to eat jelly,
Coco is tiny and furry,
He is my only worry,
He is my precious dog,
We like to go for a jog,
He is ginger in colour,
We will be together forever.

Aranie Thasan (9)
Horsenden Primary School, Greenford

Charlie

C hooses his own decisions if it's important
H isses when danger arrives
A lways finds his owner when lost
R eady to slide under my bed
L ong, lazy reptile laying on my couch
I ncredibly clever and fast doing his daily tasks
E xtraordinary pet that scares my friends a lot... that's why I like it the most!

Adam Wisowaty (10)
Horsenden Primary School, Greenford

Me And My Unicat

Me and my unicat fly to space,
We greet the stars and say hello to this dark place.
My pet can do everything, everything at once,
It can swim, fly, run, jump, jog, even dance.
We jumped on the moon and wandered around,
We need to go home and get back on the ground.
We'll say our last goodbyes,
And *whoosh! Zam! Crash! Boom!* Off we fly.

Jana Alhrouk (10)
Horsenden Primary School, Greenford

Angel The Pup

My pup Angel has eyes as blue as the sky itself,
Her hair is as white as snow can be,
She loves playing around with her chew toy,
When we play catch, she can jump and flip over,
And catch the ball in her mouth,
But best of all, she makes a good, snuggly friend,
She's sassy and furry, cute and cuddly,
She may be tiny, but she's adorable.

Cyrus Parangi (9)
Horsenden Primary School, Greenford

Frosty Mopsy

Glowing eyes like the crystal sky melting like icebergs
Wings flapping up and down like a bee buzzing in the coldness, freezing with one flap,
Claws sharpening in every take off in the freezing smoke, making him more ready,
Sharp teeth frighten his friends away in a flash of lightning,
But when he is alone, he is lazy and full of sharpening pain.

Julia Bielecka (9)
Horsenden Primary School, Greenford

Billy And Willy The Super Spectacular Dogs!

Another amazing day,
The glimmering sun shines.
Willy and Billy were besties,
Who could not be separated.
Lived in the countryside,
They were born with powers.
Willy's powers were speed mode and invincibility!
Billy's were speed mode and camouflage.
They used their powers carefully,
And worked together!

Nadia Przybyszewska (11)
Horsenden Primary School, Greenford

Bob The Fat Cat Like A Fridge

Bob is like a fridge,
At least he doesn't live on a bridge!
He is the type of cat,
That likes to have a chat.
When he is in the bathroom,
The world turns into doom.
He has eight long legs,
And obviously never begs.
"Come down!" would shout his owners,
He doesn't forget about his manners.

David Ogiela (10)
Horsenden Primary School, Greenford

Cruby The Creepster

Cruby the creepster goes out at night,
Though he will give you a fright,
Sometimes he can be very nice.
Don't get on his bad side, you will regret it,
And the kids who have seen him will never forget it.
Told you what to do, don't disobey,
But I've seen you at night, get ready to play.

Niti Upadhyay (11)
Horsenden Primary School, Greenford

Chuck Chip Chick

Chuck Chip Chick's favourite food is chips,
Chip Chick Chuck goes *cluck, cluck, cluck,*
Chuck Chip Chick fell off a cliff,
Chip Chick Chuck floated in a flick,
Now Chuck Chip Chick was super-duper fit,
Chuck Chip Chick will be a superhero who is a...
Chick!

Faye Mushatat (10)
Horsenden Primary School, Greenford

The Incredible Gaming Snake

The harmless, legless reptile
Hissing on the mic
Curly, carelessly resting on the chair
Deadly, dangerous attack on the controller
With a frightening tongue
A warm-blooded snake in motion
Alert! Alert!
Jaw-dropping win
Scaly-skinned snake win.

Aarav Shah (10)
Horsenden Primary School, Greenford

My Dog Sam

S am is a very small, yet clever dog, his fur is very fluffy
A dditionally, he has adorable and cute eyes. His legs are very quick and extraordinary
M ainly his collar is made out of gold and diamonds. Sadly, Sam only has one, but can still do incredible things.

Vibishan Kamalahasan (10)
Horsenden Primary School, Greenford

Camo Cat

Camo cat, camo cat,
Camo cat is a camouflaging cat.
Camo cat, camo cat,
Camo cat has no hat.
Camo cat, camo cat,
Camo cat shall know that.
Camo cat, camo cat,
Camo cat runs that fast.
Camo cat, camo cat,
Camo cat is a cat!

Atiya Stachowiak (10)
Horsenden Primary School, Greenford

Dangerous Cat

Don't go near Cassy,
She is very sassy.
She sleeps on something lumpy,
Which makes her very grumpy!
She's too dangerous
To be generous.
Cassy is 50% crazy
And 50% lazy.
She's far too wild,
To be near a child.

Maria Danilczyk (10)
Horsenden Primary School, Greenford

My Amazing Puppy!

P erfect dog, a shining star
U ltimate cuteness glittering on his face
P eaceful, mindful of positive, calm thoughts
P assionate tricks are trained to be on stage
Y outh is his hazel eyes, full of wonder.

Lucy-Sophie Gharapetian (10)
Horsenden Primary School, Greenford

Robo Doggy

Robo Doggy is half-cyborg, he is,
Likes being patted, but hates being slapped.
He is cute but wise,
He's tiny but playful.
What an extraordinary pet!
Never terrifying, always happy!
Always coming to greet you with joy.

Ahmed Muhday (10)
Horsenden Primary School, Greenford

Thug Cat

He is a black cat and he likes to rap,
He does rap battles in a crazy part of London,
And he beats people at rapping,
But on the streets he is known as Thug Cat,
But when he gives you a tip or two,
He will be wiser than a pig.

Yasmine Mrimou-Cahill (11)
Horsenden Primary School, Greenford

Libby The Spy Cat

Libby the spy cat,
She's dangeorus and clever,
Libby the spy cat,
She's cute, but don't be fooled,
Libby the spy cat,
She's ferocious and furry,
Libby the spy cat,
She'll gobble you up for dinner!

Aaliya Bhachu (10)
Horsenden Primary School, Greenford

Turtle

T urtles are slow and steady
U ses its shell to hide
R oughs and scuffs through the leaves
T hrough the sea, it gently glides
L umpy and bumpy, patterned shell
E yes closing as night falls.

Thayan Meisuria (9)
Horsenden Primary School, Greenford

Pelly The Parrot

P elly the parrot pecking on a carrot
E nthusiastically all day
L icking her lips as she wiggles her hips
L oving life as she sways, moving her way
Y o, yo, yo, it's Pelly the parrot!

Hibba Ashraf (10)
Horsenden Primary School, Greenford

Fish

F ree from the bowl and into the flowing stream
I guess nobody wanted me, so it would seem
S mall bits of plastic, cans, branches and leaves
H ope one day everyone recycles so that I can breathe.

Ezzah Maqsood (9)
Horsenden Primary School, Greenford

Franky

F ranky is a five-month-old puppy
R eally adorable and sweet
A brave, smart dog
N ot going to let you down
K ind and respectful
Y ellowish eyes with black.

Eryk Ficek (10)
Horsenden Primary School, Greenford

Funny Clowns, Funny Clowns

Funny clowns, funny clowns,
Jumping around, jumping around,
Sometimes funny, sometimes making faces,
Funny clowns, funny clowns,
Spinning around, spinning around,
Funny clowns, funny clowns.

Natalie Malwic (10)
Horsenden Primary School, Greenford

Graficorn

He's a puppycorn.
Graficorn is a very cute puppycorn.
He brings out the trash,
Plays with the bats.
Graficorn is fantastically furry
And a little bit lazy
And majestically merry.

Julia Zamorska (9)
Horsenden Primary School, Greenford

Harry The Hamster

H iding in his cage
A cting weirdly climbing his cage
R unning up and down our legs
R olling around acting dead
Y awning like he just woke up.

Igor Szewczyk (9)
Horsenden Primary School, Greenford

My Leon

L eon loves to play every day
E ats a lot and never stops
O nce in a while, he will whine
N evertheless, he is my Leon.

Aria-Niaya Varsani (9)
Horsenden Primary School, Greenford

My Little Dog

C ute in any way
O verreacting with aggression
C heerful for long walks
O n all occasions messy.

Jan Worytkiewicz (9)
Horsenden Primary School, Greenford

The Rapping Dog

My dog is no ordinary one,
He has a voice like none,
He can rap better than Drake,
And yet he hates the taste of cake.

Ali Abdul-Saheb (9)
Horsenden Primary School, Greenford

Lilka The Dog

My dog is cute
He doesn't like fruit
But he likes dog food
He's always in a good mood.

Jakub Lawniczak (9)
Horsenden Primary School, Greenford

My Parrot

My parrot talks a lot
Nuts and fruit is what he eats
He has vividly coloured clawed feet.

Ruqayyah Alowdany (10)
Horsenden Primary School, Greenford

Sam The Talking Dog

Sam is a dog and he likes to talk,
He mostly talks when he goes for a walk.
If you ever see Sam, watch out for his tail,
It wags so hard it could bang in a nail!
He gives you a paw to get your attention,
Then utters a word that I really mustn't mention.
He has a smooth brown coat that blends with his eyes,
And a mad sense of humour when he's hanging with the guys.
Sam is always hungry and he loves his meat,
But secretly it's cake he loves to eat!
If you hear a husky voice that's a little bit 'ruff',
Look out for Sam doing his strange stuff!

Rory Ranson (10)
Ludgvan Community Primary School, Ludgvan

My Peculiar Pet

P lease respect my peculiar pet
E very inch of this creature is filled with tonnes of love and joy
C ome and meet my pawsome pet
U ncover every surprise
L ovable with an orange fishy tail
I must show its human smile
A ll within a cat-like kitty
R iddled with monumental flamingo wings

P ets are the best, especially peculiar ones
E ven you could end up with a pet
T reasure every snuggle
S o treat them the same way as a baby.

Kyla Curnow (10)
Ludgvan Community Primary School, Ludgvan

My Special Pet

Her hair is long and glossy
She can also be quite bossy
She loves a sparkling rainbow
And eating delicious hay in her favourite meadow
Her colourful body is full of cuddles
But sometimes she gets in a clumsy muddle
She runs as fast as a speeding train
And flies to the clouds amongst the planes
Her tail is pink and full of curls
She loves to eat a chocolate Twirl
I've got to admit she's an awesome friend
But sometimes she can drive me round the bend.

Poppy Jacobs (9)
Ludgvan Community Primary School, Ludgvan

Monster Dog

M onster dog is as lazy as a sloth
O n his bed, he sleeps all day through
N ever cleans up
S uper clever like a fox though
T he monster dog is as gentle as a kitten
E njoys being stroked and
R ed, yellow and blue are his colours

D igging in his sleep is totally his thing
O nly don't give him broccoli, it turns him green
G o on, meet him, why don't you?

Sofia Collins (10)
Ludgvan Community Primary School, Ludgvan

The Dragon-Spider

The dragon-spider isn't a liar,
It flies around and breathes some fire,
Then it goes from town to town not making a sound,
The wings are little and don't touch the ground.

The two-tailed, four-winged dragon-spider,
Is the size of your palm and not any wider,
Two bites can kill you, so you better steer clear,
These peculiar pets are somewhere near here.

Abby Long (9)
Ludgvan Community Primary School, Ludgvan

Crurtool

C reepy little Crurtool resides in the jungle
R etreats to his cave while his friends squabble
U nique and powerful Crurtool might be
R obust, brave and strong is he
T ogether is better than being alone
O nwards and upwards is the way we must go
O ut in the cold hunting for food
L ovely jubbly, chicken stew.

Emily Basher (10)
Ludgvan Community Primary School, Ludgvan

Squeatle BFF

A Kennings poem

Lazy sleeper
Meat eater
Rabbit hunter
Athletic jumper
Spotty fur preener
Vacuum cleaner
Lap sitter
Nose licker
Arm nuzzler
Cute cuddler
Squeaky purrer
Bushy-tailed furrer
Cheeky scratcher
String ball catcher
Mane wearer
Blue-eyed starer
Love giver
Best friend forever...

Squeatle!

Gracie Dyer (9)
Ludgvan Community Primary School, Ludgvan

Flying Tiger

F lies through trees
L oves swooping around
Y ou won't believe it
I n the sky or on the ground
N ow you see it, now you don't
G o flying tiger

T he flying tiger is amazing
I t can walk and fly
G o, go, go
E xtraordinary
R emarkable.

Alfie Healey (9)
Ludgvan Community Primary School, Ludgvan

Cool Peter

C ats are bonkers
O f course they are
O nly Peter is peculiar though
L ong beak and legs

P retty amazing tail
E ven webbed feet!
T en red whiskers
E veryone adores cool Peter
R eady to meet you!

Margo Dumbleton (9)
Ludgvan Community Primary School, Ludgvan

Flying Dogs

Happy, smiley, jumpy dogs leaping through the air,
Giving everyone hugs like they just don't care,
When you walk down the street you will jump up with a scare,
Because there is a two-winged dog just standing there,
So if you have a dog, just be aware.

Riley Le Seelleur (10)
Ludgvan Community Primary School, Ludgvan

Hammy The Hamster

H ammy is happy
A dorable and cute
M essy and marvellous
S leeps in his blue home
T iny, lame and ginger
E xtraordinary, energetic in his wheel
R uns round and round his blue home.

Luke Scott (9)
Ludgvan Community Primary School, Ludgvan

Bonnie The Unidog

I have a peculiar pet
It is a unidog
It can fly like a jet
And can see in the fog
It is rainbow-coloured and pink
Its name is Bonnie
My peculiar pet.

Jessica Townson (9)
Ludgvan Community Primary School, Ludgvan

Magical Caticorn

M agically Caticorn soars through the sky with her wings
A s she lays down, she dreams of bathing in a warm bath
G ently at night, she climbs on the bed without disturbing me
I f I could, I would hug her, I would, but I can never catch her
C aticorn is as lazy as an old dog
A s she lays down, she purrs loudly
L uckily, Caticorn has a never-ending life unlike other cats

C aticorn is ginger with white patterns on her fur
A s I gaze out the window, I see Caticorn playing in the clouds
T erribly at night she catches defenceless birds and brings it as a surprise
I love Caticorn because she is so fluffy like a blanket
C aticorn is half unicorn, half cat
O ddly, Caticorn has a lion's roar as loud as a siren

R unning at night gives Caticorn exercise which makes her skinny
N o one likes it when Caticorn flies away beyond the clouds because they can't see her.

Lilly Ella Jerram (9)
Simms Cross Primary School, Widnes

Hocto-Snake In The Sky, One Of The Coolest Guys!

Hocto-Snake,
Is not the best of names,
But I'm sure there's a creature out there,
That has exactly the same.

What's a Hocto-Snake?
You might be asking,
Well, helping, flying,
But mostly exterminating.

What does it eat?
Well, only steak,
Because it rhymes with his name,
Hocto-Snake.

Its name has octo,
For eight snakes together,
And the ho makes it fly,
And also means helicopter.

Although he is cruel,
He is also polite,
But he has a problem,
It's his excellent flight.

Everyone is jealous of him,
As he can be heard,
From over a mile,
And can fly better than a bird.

How high can he fly?
Higher than a vulture?
Well, he can go to space, Mars,
And climb the tallest structure.

For a change,
He has two friends,
Bocto and Socto
And this is the end.

Salim Ghounay (11)
Simms Cross Primary School, Widnes

The Wardrobe Thief

Yesterday, I bought a pony named Sparkle
A very adorable creature
Everyone admired her beauty
Along with her crazy feature...

It was only last night when she escaped
I was eating some Snickers
When I turned around and...
Saw her in my knickers!

I was ever so shocked
Does she have secret hands?
When I looked again...
She was wearing my headbands.

I woke up this morning, looked out my window
Sparkle was driving my sports car
When I looked again...
She was wearing my sports bra

Last night, I got a sweet stuck in my tooth
It was a lollipop
When I yelled for my pony...
She was wearing my crop top

My pony may take my clothes
But trust me, she's the best
I love my pony to the moon and back
Even though she's different from the rest.

Neave Edwards (10)
Simms Cross Primary School, Widnes

Jumping Jax

A little puppy about a month old,
Three-quarters chihuahua, Jack Russell too,
You would never know,
That this little puppy can jump to the moon,
In the blink of an eye.
Once a little boy was taking him for a walk,
When he blinked, the dog was gone,
All that was left was a tower of wind,
So looked up and he saw a speck in the air.
When he came back down, he made a crater,
He bounced from and back,
The moon in less than a second.
When he landed, he made a crater,
He bounced from and back,
The moon in less than a second.
When he landed, he vaporised the grass,
His paws were covered in ice,
As he had gone to space.
The boy was confused,
So the dog acted like nothing had happened.

Bobby Dunning (10)
Simms Cross Primary School, Widnes

The Donkeycorn

Have you ever heard of a donkeycorn?
Tail of grey and a glittery horn,
Fluffy, big, white wings,
She can't rap but she can sing,
At night she flies me up very high,
And off we go, we take to the sky,
Down we go back to the land,
And we snuggle up in the sand,
Back we go home to bed,
She goes back in the shed,
In the shed it's dark and grey,
But she knows tomorrow is going to be a good day,
In the morning we go to the farm,
When we go there she causes lots of harm,
Her horn once got stuck in someone's bum,
And the girl had to call her mum,
My donkeycorn was upset and sad,
I say it's okay to be mad,
We go to bed hoping for the best day to come yet.

Ava Grace Gatcliffe (10)
Simms Cross Primary School, Widnes

Clover The Tap Dancing Penguin

Last week we adopted a penguin
Then we brought him home
My mother gave him food
Then left him all alone.

Yesterday my penguin came
My knee is where he sat
Then he started dancing
Dancing on my lap.

I stood gasping there
Gasping with surprise
Yet he kept dancing
Dancing to the skies.

That penguin is still dancing
That chubby little thing
It all got a lot stranger
When my friend's dog began to sing.

My penguin is dancing
Dancing throughout the land
It only took a moment for
Him to start the land.

My penguin was playing,
Playing my favourite tune
It only took a moment
To make the ladies swoon.

Spencer Smith-Underwood (10)
Simms Cross Primary School, Widnes

Funky The Flying Donkey

Yo, my name is Funky
Yeah, I'm really cool,
I have a big house
With an extremely cool room.

I like tap dancing
Yeah, that's my jam,
I am very colourful
And I like to eat ham.

I have a secret talent
That I use when I'm bored,
Beautiful wings come from my back
Which my friends and I think is very whack.

I am lucky to live in my owner's bed
All day I love to sleep,
Most days I go round in my car
I don't know why I don't fly - it's not very far.

Overall, I am a lazy donkey
I don't use my talent very well,

I eat, sleep and fly, then repeat
That's just who I am.

Miley Fowler (10)
Simms Cross Primary School, Widnes

The Frog That Can't Croak, But Can Rap

My name is Greeny and I'm the best
I'm always super tired because I never rest
I have slimy, bumpy skin so I'm really cool
And if you don't like me, you're a big fool

I cannot croak because I'm a big bloke
I run around and go round and round
I travel the world because I'm super bored
Can you please be my friend? I need to have more

I stink of mud, but I'm full of gold
And if you travel with me I'll do as I'm told
I'm green like Shrek and I live on a shipwreck
I sleep on a deck and I wake up as a wreck
Now I think it's pretty clear that I'm the best of the best.

Pippa Nelly Magee (10)
Simms Cross Primary School, Widnes

Mischievous Lucy

Lucy the mischievous cat
Oh no!
She spilt all the milk on the floor
Lucy!
Up on the couch she ripped the cushions
Next was my pillow
I gave her the devil eyes
She just got up and walked off
I called her Fussy Cat
Layla, my cat's friend, is a fat cat
Who never gets up from his sleep
If only he played out with his friends!
My cat has a bike
She goes vroom, vroom up and down a hill
I can't catch her, she is fast
Boom!
She smashes into a lamp post
Oh no, let's hope tomorrow is good and better than today!

Emily B (10)
Simms Cross Primary School, Widnes

The Rapping Donkey

Yo, my name is Lil' D,
And I'm mostly grey.
I like to sing,
And I also eat hay.

When I bust ma moves,
People say I'm bendy.
I cannot really sing,
But my rap is hip and trendy.

I'm walking down the street,
Everyone knows my name.
There's not many donkeys,
With rapping as their game.

Around my neck I wear,
A golden chain.
Like Cardi B,
My raps are insane.

At the end of every day,
I lay down to rest.
As rapping donkeys go,
I'm certainly the best.

Drops the microphone...
Peace out!

Alivia Riley (10)
Simms Cross Primary School, Widnes

Shell-less Turtle

I have a pet named Myrtle
She is my baby turtle
What is odd about her
She looks like a bottom
Some people may call her undressed
But the fact is, she's just shell-less
She's a trendy, bendy turtle
She has a yellow streak I painted on her back
I think she could be from the USA
'Cos she loves to eat Jell-O
She eats it with peanut butter
Like an American fellow
She's blue with yellow stripes on her back
Does she like to chew bubblegum? Let's try
She knew she was in double trouble
When I saw a bubble on the floor.

Nicola Palyz (11)
Simms Cross Primary School, Widnes

The Cinnamonsaur

Have you heard of a creature that smells like spice?
A green beast that is very nice,
With a white belly that is chubby and plump,
So lazy it's like a talking lump,
It's the cutest thing you ever saw,
It's the lovely, cuddly, hungry Cinnamonsaur!

The Cinnamonsaur talks with a deep baby voice,
Never takes a bath, but its skin is so moist,
Its favourite place to eat at is Taco Bell,
But when it eats it starts to smell,
It's the most peculiar thing you ever saw,
It's the lovely, cuddly, hungry Cinnamonsaur!

Frank Bussey (10)
Simms Cross Primary School, Widnes

The Amazing Sloth

If you've heard of a sloth,
Then you're sure to know that this lethargic, idle creature is really... rather... slow,
But I know a type that is as fast as a cheetah,
And if you race him then he is sure to beat ya,
He is that fast that he will never be last,
This insane species even speaks with speed,
Often he will make your ears bleed,
This friendly yellow fellow is unquestionably the best,
We want him to wear a British racing vest,
Because we know he will win gold,
You have been warned because he is bold.

Zeynur Yuseinova (10)
Simms Cross Primary School, Widnes

Bella-Pink

I have a pet called Bella-Pink
I'm crazy is what you think
'Cause she is a cat, but also a dog
She doesn't like fog
She's adorable, also tiny
I have to admit we are both sassy
She always curls up next to my left leg
Her toy is called Meg
Bella-Pink is amazing at ballet
And loves to be spooky
She loves to eat Mum's pudding, it's always a hit
But she doesn't say
She loves to do ballet
But she hates the salsa
She's super clever
She is the best pet ever.

Jessica-Lea Downey (9)
Simms Cross Primary School, Widnes

Disco Dancing Dodo

Although the dodo is extinct
A disco dancing dodo is very distinct
He might be the new Michael Jackson
Even Simon Cowell will have satisfaction

John Travolta has some competition
I told him to have a Broadway audition
Disco dancing dodo becomes a famous celebrity
Performing dances with great intensity

I wouldn't be surprised if the 70s were when he was made
As that was when disco dancing was most displayed
If you ever see a disco dancing dodo
Make sure you let him do his mojo.

Lily-Mai Graham-Brown (10)
Simms Cross Primary School, Widnes

Sclas: Snake Lizard

Feel lucky that you're not on Sclas' feasting list,
He is a snake lizard, a no emotion beast,
Are those teeth or knives?
Are those claws or spikes?
From afar, he looks like a Komodo dragon,
But no, it is a fearful monster,
Over 1000 years old and always hungry.

Raaaa!

He moves fast when he sees or smells fresh meat,
But he's mostly slow,
He is as tall as a mountain lion,
And as long as the world's longest snake,
Terrible smell and insane venom.

Zen Edison Stokes (9)
Simms Cross Primary School, Widnes

One-Eyed Cheeky Monkey!

I am a one-eyed cheeky monkey,
And Mischief is my name,
Swinging in trees and playing with bees
Is one of my favourite games,
I also like to throw rocks at people passing by,
But I accidentally slipped and one went in my eye,
I may look kind of fun with my cherry-shaped bum,
But you better think fast,
Because bananas give me gas,
And soon you will smell it in the breeze,
So next time you're in the jungle
And hear a bash and rumble,
Remember I am a one-eyed cheeky monkey.

Eleanor Forshaw (10)
Simms Cross Primary School, Widnes

Frake The Unusual Frog

I have a pet called Frake,
Half frog, half snake,
His body is long and lean,
But his head is fat and green,
He's the strangest creature to have ever been seen,
He's slimy to the touch,
But I love him very much,
He talks with a croak and a bit of a hiss,
If you think he's strange, you should see his sis,
Her name is Snackog,
Half snake, half frog,
Her body's green with funny little feet not very long,
Her head is like a snake with a stretchy tongue.

Faith Pitt (10)
Simms Cross Primary School, Widnes

The Wasp That Went Mad

This is the story about a wasp that went mad,
But in fact, he was my lad,
His name was Wasper,
But then he was the imposter,
We used to have lots of fun,
And he would make us a bun (wasp candy),
He was angry one time,
And he tortured the Queen,
But then he went insane,
He wrecked the house,
No one wanted to be around,
Not even a mouse,
His name was Wasper,
Then he was mad,
I wanted to help him,
But I couldn't even if I could.

Archie Smith Underwood (10)
Simms Cross Primary School, Widnes

The Beast In The Woods

M anticor is a human scorpion lion
A nd it is a ferocious beast, it could probably kill a python
N ext it could probably kill a ferocious dinosaur or lion
T he Manticor is the beast of the woods and the creature is amazing
I t may as well have its own business
C rocodiles could not even kill it, it's unstoppable
O n its adventures, you always get a treasure
R on is a person who got treasure on a mission.

Jayden Robinson (9)
Simms Cross Primary School, Widnes

Mo The Search Cat

Mo used to be a normal cat
He always slept and never went out
Sometimes he ate until he became the size of a house
And when he hunted, he found the odd mouse
He never fought, he was too lazy
And if he did, the ground would be shaky

I woke up this morning
With Mo waiting to be fed
He looked a little bit odd
Because he'd tied up a frog
I stayed up late to see the crime
And guess who I saw?
Mo high in the sky.

Alfie Rowlands (10)
Simms Cross Primary School, Widnes

What A Messy Alien Tiger!

What a peculiar pet,
Never touch it or you'll get a fever,
Never touch its fur, it feels like a beaver,
Its teeth are metal,
With breath as hot as a kettle,
It goes for a walk around a school,
Looking very, very cool,
It makes a sound like twisting spaghetti,
Leaving a trail of colourful confetti,
The older it gets it shrinks,
And all of a sudden it's gone with a blink.

Harry Sheehan (10)
Simms Cross Primary School, Widnes

Clive

Yesterday, my mum adopted an amazing turtle,
But little did we know he had some talents.

One day, we were out in the garden enjoying the sun,
And suddenly my little turtle wanted to have some fun.

He stood up and started to dance a jive,
He danced around the garden and gave me a high-five.

If you ever meet a turtle called Clive,
Make sure you help him dance his jive.

Alexi O'Brien
Simms Cross Primary School, Widnes

The Angry Hiss

There is a cat more dangerous than a tiger!
With great big claws (or spikes),
With sharp teeth (or is it a fang?),
His fur always pops up,
When something doesn't go his way...

Hisssss!

He can swallow mice in two seconds!
Just feel lucky, you're not on his menu,
But I've got to warn you...
Never, ever scratch him on the belly!
Ever!

Arnas Petrauskas (10)
Simms Cross Primary School, Widnes

The Troublemaker Puppy

H ow can the puppy breathe ice and fire?
O nly been on the floor
T ell you about my troublemaker puppy

P uppy, you are too cute
U p to bed now
P uppy, come for a walk
P up, you burnt my pad down
Y ou are funny

F unny, you are funny
I love my pup
R eally
E njoy my puppy.

Emily Watson (10)
Simms Cross Primary School, Widnes

Fairy Foxy

Fairy Foxy is a fairy
She loves flying around
But she is allergic to dairy
She always flies through the clouds.

She loves to sing and dance too
That is what she likes to do
Also, she has a friend called Mia Mouse
They fly around all day and night.

They are always playing together
But when her friend goes home
She feels sad and alone.

Libby Savage (10)
Simms Cross Primary School, Widnes

The Flying Fish

Flying fish never says hi,
Flying fish flies so high,
The stinking fish smells like spilt milk,
Never cleaned up, never to chase,
Never stops playing up,
Always diving in the air,
Wanting to catch food for the others to share,
Flying fish never says hi,
Flying fish flies so high,
The messy and sassy creature,
Likes the smell of strawberries.

Kelsey Willcox (10)
Simms Cross Primary School, Widnes

The Daring Kangaroo

Last night we adopted a kangaroo,
But little did we know,
This kangaroo likes giving our door a chew.

His name is Bob,
He likes to lie on logs,
Lying on them all day,
While eating his favourite hay.

I'll hop around all day,
And I'll pray all day,
Waiting for my owner to come today,
One more dance to make it a day.

Abigail Atherton (11)
Simms Cross Primary School, Widnes

Rocky The Dog

Hi, I am Rocky!
I am a doggy,
I have a bed in my shed,
I am brown like a log,
My power is fire,
You better watch out,
Or you will expire!
I set fire to my owner's bed,
And sometimes her hair on her head!
A skill that I think is nice.
I won't be able to die,
Because he will bring me back to life.

Maisie Johns (9)
Simms Cross Primary School, Widnes

The Non-Barking Unicorn Dog

My unicorn dog is a dog that doesn't bark,
Instead he howls in the park.
His eyes are blue like the shining sky
And he likes to jump up high.

My dog chomps on pie,
He caught me at the end of my eye,
And that made me cry.
His howl sounds like an owl,
This makes him sad and mad.

Grace Fowler (10)
Simms Cross Primary School, Widnes

Indigo The Turtle

- **I** ndependent as a 13-year-old
- **N** o one could ever expect a turtle with long legs
- **D** ull as the 1980's cameras
- **I** ndigo never breaks the speed limit
- **G** olden cage just like a pineapple
- **O** cean-blue sky eyes.

Joel Machell-McCann (9)
Simms Cross Primary School, Widnes

Charm The Cute, Colourful Cat!

C is for cute, colourful cat with majestic fur!
H is for helpful, happy, healthy life!
A is for amazing, astonishing personality!
R is for respectful, sweet manners!
M is for marvellous, majestic eyes!

Jay Jay Rodgers (10)
Simms Cross Primary School, Widnes

My Monkey And Me

M agnificent creatures, they are magical
O ne is his favourite number
N aughty monkey is on a time-out branch
K evin is his name
E ars as big as saucers
Y ou have a monkey for a pet.

Patrick McMahon (9)
Simms Cross Primary School, Widnes

Kevin The Monkey

M agnificent creature
O ne is his favourite number
N aughty monkey on the time-out branch
K evin is his name
E ars as big as saucers
Y ou wouldn't like a monkey for a pet.

Megan Willcox-Collington (9), Maisy Owens (9), Patrick, Harry Tiernan (9) & Robert Bowen (9)
Simms Cross Primary School, Widnes

My Marvellous Phoenix

My marvellous phoenix comes to play when no one is looking,
He's as bright as a ball of fire,
When he flies he makes an inferno mess,
He flies high above the sky,
Leaving behind a fiery trail across the sky.

Logan Dunn (10)
Simms Cross Primary School, Widnes

The One And Only Bella!

B ella is a friendly dog
E ating when she is hungry doesn't bother you
L oving and kind, makes sure you're safe
L ike a fluffy pillow
A lways keeps you safe, no matter what.

Kaitlin Dolman (9)
Simms Cross Primary School, Widnes

The Ender Dragon

Its purple eyes as bright as the night,
That shine like daylight,
His pointy teeth as sharp as a sword,
Cut through a human like a butter knife,
A colossal tail as big as a whale,
He hails from the end.

Leon Walton (10)
Simms Cross Primary School, Widnes

The One And Only Bella Budgie

B ella is sleepy like an owl
E lla is so cute and I was crying
L eaving her bed and me alone at home
L ooking at her bed while going away
A lways going back, back and back.

Phoebe Batty (9)
Simms Cross Primary School, Widnes

The One And Only Sassy

S he is a very sleepy dog
A lways makes sure you are safe
S he is very lazy and looks like a Dalmatian
S he loves her beef and tomato food
Y ou will love her.

Alana-Louise (10)
Simms Cross Primary School, Widnes

Poppy

P oppy is peculiar
O h no, what has she done now?
P eeking in on secrets
P eacocks are one sly creature
Y ay, should never try and beat one.

Jamie King (10)
Simms Cross Primary School, Widnes

The Lazy Pup!

Have you ever heard of a lazy pup this lazy?
Lazy-Loo she is as lazy as anything,
But she is very, very clever,
I will tell you why.
I'm homeschooled and whenever I get an answer right,
She writes it down carefully!
She should be called Clever-Clue,
But she would have hated that ugly name.
"Lazy-Loo," my dad said.
"Woof!" Treat time!
Anyway, I'm Leah and I live in a crooked house,
It's very ugly.
I live with my mum, my dad and Lazy-Loo!
We live here 'cause my mum was silly to buy this £1000 pound old house!
I'm so angry!
I loved my old house, it was beautiful!
Gotta go, off now, see ya later! Bye!
"Lacy-Loo, say bye!"
"Woof, woof!" said Lacy-Loo!

Leah Overett (9)
St Paul's Catholic Primary School, Cheshunt

Banana City

Colourful city,
The yellow, wheaty grass,
Plunging palm trees,
Whistling wind,
It is the perfect place for Millie the party monkey.
She may look adorable,
But really she's sassy and lazy,
Shhh, don't tell her,
Jumps around all over the palm trees. *Snap!*
There goes another tree,
Silly Millie,
Oh, oops! I did it again!
Where's mischievous Millie going now?
Here we are again,
She's starting to dance on Yellow Mustard Lake,
Cheeky monkey,
You know you're not allowed,
Crash! Ouch! I fell,
Millie the monkey,
Millie the crazy monkey.

Georgia Cannell (10)
St Paul's Catholic Primary School, Cheshunt

The Colourful And Lazy Dog

My colourful and lazy dog,
He loves to be lazy and sleep all the time.
What a nice time!
My dog was like a stick,
From not eating his dinner when I made it,
I always say to myself,
Why don't you eat your food?
I have an idea,
I am going to call you Lazy Dog,
That is an amazing name.
Within the blink of an eye,
The lazy dog got up and what was he doing?
Eating his dinner!
Oh my, he is finally eating.
His furry scales scare me to pieces,
I don't like it.
Wow, he is so messy for a dog like him,
I know, let me take him for a walk.

Madison Pell (10)
St Paul's Catholic Primary School, Cheshunt

Lograulour

He's sneaky and wild like a log,
Run with the wind like a slippy young log!
Monkey he is with his clever, clever brain,
You can see his radiant blue eyes from a distance,
He mixes with the brown of the trees and black of the night,
In his free time, he likes to be lazy,
You find him in the forest of magic,
It's hard to tame him with his speed,
He's very gentle because he's so tiny,
All you can hear is the gentle wind,
So quick he can summon a tornado,
He's scared of everything,
He can be very messy though,
He's a marvellous new pet!

Damian Chudy (10)
St Paul's Catholic Primary School, Cheshunt

The Baking Alicorn

Have you ever seen a Baking Alicorn?
They have furry scales and are extremely clever,
But yet they are very, very messy,
This incredible creature is blue with furry scales,
And a unicorn horn to top it all off.

They live in a wild forest and bake at a dark blue counter,
Many try to get past this creature, but yet all fail,
With speed faster than lightning,
Flashing down from the stormy clouds.

Everybody tries to steal its best recipes,
But yet all unfortunately fail,
Its name is the Baking Alicorn,
Have you seen one?

Laura Rice (9)
St Paul's Catholic Primary School, Cheshunt

The Dancing Puppy!

Have you heard of a dancing puppy?
With a cute face like the cuteness of a newborn baby,
And eyes as big as a marble,
Would you come up to the puppy and feel its furry skin?

Have you heard of a dancing puppy?
With elegant dancing skills like the elegant swans,
Would you join in with the puppy or just walk away?

Have you heard of a dancing puppy?
With the softest ears ever and a fluffy tail,
Would you go up to the adorable puppy and tell it how amazing it was when it was dancing,
Or just think you're imagining it?

Tiara Oke (9)
St Paul's Catholic Primary School, Cheshunt

Jack The Arsenal Dog

Have you ever seen a talking dog called Jack?
With small, white, bright teeth like the shining sun,
And gold fur that is fluffy and soft.

Have you ever seen a talking dog?
That plays sports like football, basketball and athletics,
It has a head like a round, silver ball,
He can also climb walls and walk on walls,
Also, it can jump incredibly high,
He can literally jump over the clouds,
It is sometimes dangerous when you annoy him,
Or when someone is in danger, would you stop?
To talk to this clever and incredible dog?

Noel Ranasinghe (10)
St Paul's Catholic Primary School, Cheshunt

Singing Snow Leopard!

Have you ever seen a singing snow leopard?
That has a singing voice like Ariana Grande's,
And eyes as blue as the bright, blue sky,
Would you cry or scream?

Have you ever seen a singing snow leopard?
With paws as agile as ballerinas dancing on stage,
And teeth as sharp as a knife,
Would you smile and stare?

Have you ever seen a singing snow leopard?
With a tail as gentle as a snake slithering up your arm,
And fur as thick as snow in the winter,
What would you do if you caught sight of one?

Ava Rose Guy (9)
St Paul's Catholic Primary School, Cheshunt

Turbo The Cheetah

Deep in the forest there lives a starving cheetah,
If you go in there hiking you'd better beware.
Someday, perhaps, he'll run so fast,
That the rivers, lakes, seas and oceans,
Will fly out of their spots.
He crawls but he's small,
Turbo glazed at the reindeer as prey,
But there a large bear leans to its prey,
He goes into the large bear,
And barges into his cosy, furry fur,
And can't get over his fur.
Suddenly, something pinched him,
And ran away as fast as he could to safety.

Daniel Marinov (10)
St Paul's Catholic Primary School, Cheshunt

In The Forest

Sneaking into the bottle-green forest,
A lick of silver in the depths of the shadows,
Under the soft glow of the moon,
Knowing prey will be here soon.

With effortless grace, it leapt over logs and streams,
Emerald eyes, fixing them on what lay ahead,
On a pebble grey squirrel frozen in stark terror,
Then in a clumsy haste disappears up a tree.

Growling and howling, writhing with rage,
Silently retreats into the forest,
Melting away into the night,
Never to be seen again.

Kayra Saffet (11)
St Paul's Catholic Primary School, Cheshunt

Roarsome

R oarsome is my name
O h, my beak is gigantic, plucking my meat
A nd I am ferocious, I am starved
R oaming through the Forest of Deen
S limy, messy, grumpy, lazy
O h, my hair is as sharp as knives
M y deep blue eyes look into your soul, searching deeper and deeper
E ntering the land of the king.

I am extraordinary,
If I cross you, you better beware,
I am feathery, I am clawed,
I am wild, ferocious,
I can't be tamed.

Ruairí Hickey (10)
St Paul's Catholic Primary School, Cheshunt

The Singing, Acrobatic Dog

Have you ever seen my really unique pet?

Well, let me tell you about her!

My amazing pet dog is called the singing and acrobatic dog.
It does fabulous flips like backflips, front flips, back handsprings and much more.
How amazing is that?

My pet is so cute that you would want to steal her or take her from me.
It is an adorable, amazing, little puppy Labrador.

My dog is so super sassy, so I would say to be careful, because you might fall in love with her.

Valentina Kasa (9)
St Paul's Catholic Primary School, Cheshunt

Tig The Extraordinary Animal

In the sand it walks,
It stares, squeaks and sprints in the wind,
Its chocolate coloured eyes stampeding to the bushes,
As the sunset goes down,
He eats the earthworms,
Smashing its beak into the ground,
When the sun goes down,
It crunches its legs into its body and lies down,
Slowly drifting away into the imaginary world,
It is an ostrich that looks fierce in the pit of sand,
Running wild in the zoo,
Everyone gazing at the feathered wings,
And its long neck.

Louie Wallis (10)
St Paul's Catholic Primary School, Cheshunt

Haily The Flexible Unicorn

Have you ever seen a flexible unicorn?
Who can do the splits, amazing or what?
With wings as graceful as swans.

Have you ever seen a flexible unicorn?
She can do cartwheels, round-offs,
Whatever you like, right in front of your eyes.

Have you ever seen a flexible unicorn?
She is very smart, I ask her to get me,
Tea and Coke from across the road.

Be careful, she is very dangerous,
If you talk bad about her,
Oh no, she heard me, *argh!*

Joanne Onyearugbulem (9)
St Paul's Catholic Primary School, Cheshunt

Slithering Snake

I have a long body, I like it a lot.
But somedays I look at the other animals and wish I could trot.

I have no arms or legs, not even an ear,
and I do not bite, don't worry my dear.

Okay, that was a lie, but I have to admit, it was really funny,
yay, six o'clock, that means it's time to catch a bunny.

Why are people so scared of me?
I always feel really lonely.

Do you know who I am?
Do not make a mistake or I'll catch it on cam.

Chloe Sritharan (10)
St Paul's Catholic Primary School, Cheshunt

The Flexible, Singing Unicorn

Have you ever seen my peculiar pet?
She is called the flexible singing uni!
She is sassy, colourful and extraordinary!
She has a voice as marvellous as a pop star,
And is as flexible as an elastic band.

Have you ever seen my peculiar pet?
She is very popular and sassy.
With a gorgeous, glamorous horn,
That is neon and unique!
Her tail is as fluffy as a Pomeranian,
And is so amazing and adorable!

Do you want to meet my precious, peculiar pet now?

Honor Hart (9)
St Paul's Catholic Primary School, Cheshunt

The Lazy Grass Eater

I am a horse,
A very hairy horse,
People see me every day,
But don't seem to notice me,
There's one thing I like to do,
Which is to eat a handful of grass!
I also like to look at nature,
It grows all around us,
But people don't notice it,
I don't like to feed myself,
Because I get my owner to do it for me,
I give people lifts.
But one slight breath and I'll give you a kick!
I am a very lazy horse,
I am a horse!

Leo Alfano (10)
St Paul's Catholic Primary School, Cheshunt

The Bear In The Breeze

Hidden in the tall, pine, olive green trees there is a bear,
Each time he thumps his paws on the snow his footsteps dissolve,
He is always lurking in the dark,
Whenever he breathes in and out, plumes rise into the chilled air,
His fur is a crowd of small river snakes,
He always throws his body into the shadows,
Whenever he approaches all humans they look petrified,
He has pitch-black eyes that glare at the darkness,
The silence deafens,
Are you scared?

Amelia Sobejko (10)
St Paul's Catholic Primary School, Cheshunt

The Raving Crab

I went to the beach,
On the floor laid a bottle of bleach.
As I picked it up,
The sand started to rise,
To my surprise, after the rise,
I heard a bang and then I got flung,
After I hit the ground,
I woke up with a frown,
And my skin tanned brown.
And in the distance,
I saw a colossal stampede of crabs.
One of them grabbed a phone and started to play music,
Their crabby feet moving to the beat.
Please help me in this burning heat.

Lennon Connolly (10)
St Paul's Catholic Primary School, Cheshunt

The Vicious Eelium

Have you ever seen a crossbreed eel and helium?
Well, it can go to phenomenal speeds, 10,000mph,
It uses its speed to scare the ferocious predators.
It eats fish farts to gain air for its helium,
Don't get fooled,
It can kill a great white with one mystical bite.
It's so intelligent, it's magic,
It's 80 times smarter than us,
Its teeth are like a piranha,
Also, it can grow up to 16 foot long,
And its weight is ten tonnes.

Cayden Desouza-Singh (9)
St Paul's Catholic Primary School, Cheshunt

Spotless Sammy

The great giant Sammy who has no spots,
Unlike most giraffes who have lots and lots,
A very grumpy creature with enormous ears,
So when everyone talks, he always hears,
He's as scary as a lion for he's ever so large,
And you better step aside or you will get barged,
He's very strange, Sammy, all alone,
With his ears the shape of an ice cream cone,
He's always sad about being so lonely,
Why is everyone so scared of me?

Ailbe Coleman (10)
St Paul's Catholic Primary School, Cheshunt

The Acrobatic Rabbit

Have you ever seen an acrobatic rabbit?
With adorable eyes like giant footballs,
And teeth as wild as a bear,
Would you stop and stare?

Have you ever seen an acrobatic rabbit?
With creative, colourful, furry fur,
And a tail as elegant as a magical mermaid,
What would you do?

Have you ever seen an acrobatic rabbit?
With extraordinary paws like a trampoline,
And a scaly spine all down her back,
Imagine that!

Isabella Clack (9)
St Paul's Catholic Primary School, Cheshunt

The Partying Ponies

Have you ever seen a partying pony?
You probably think they're not real,
But what if I told you they were real.
They have bright rainbow horns,
Unlike an ordinary pony,
Also, they have graceful pink fur,
And a delicate white tail,
They're also crazy and party all day, all night,
They're so mad they will make your ears bleed,
You can find them in the high clouds in the sky,
Do you dare to spend a night with them?

Jordan Mutsau (9)
St Paul's Catholic Primary School, Cheshunt

Tilly The Sassy Skunk

Tilly is the sassiest skunk you will ever meet,
She even has her own seat!
Get too close and she will spray,
As she thinks of horses eating hay,
Tilly tries to get a tan,
But the sun just ran,
Why is she so stinky?
Her best friend is called Tinkie,
But once she has had a bath,
She will be a laugh,
Tilly goes to the spa,
But then everyone screams, "Argh!"
Maybe I should've got a dog!

Sophia Beckford (10)
St Paul's Catholic Primary School, Cheshunt

Parrots

I'm a parrot,
Party parrot,
Always playing around parrot,
Dancing around like a crazy parrot,
A very unusual and strange parrot,
I'm a parrot,
A party parrot,
I'm a play-with-all-the-animals parrot,
A very, very playful parrot,
Not careful, not a responsible parrot,
I'm a parrot,
A party parrot,
Always messing around parrot,
Not your average parrot,
I'm a parrot.

Mia Frangione (10)
St Paul's Catholic Primary School, Cheshunt

Polly The Penguin

I'm Polly the penguin,
I'm also very furry!
My eyesight is blurry,
I'm marvellous and adorable,
I'm clever and agile,
But that doesn't mean I am not wild,
I am sassy,
I'm colourful,
But beware,
If you go to Antarctica,
You'll meet the happy Polly the penguin,
I like to meet people,
I wear sunglasses with an ice cream in my hand,
For I'm Polly the penguin.

Dominika Guszpit (10)
St Paul's Catholic Primary School, Cheshunt

The Dancing Shark!

Have you ever seen a dancing shark?
With teeth as sharp as swords,
And eyes as big as tennis balls,
Would you run or stay?

Have you ever seen a dancing shark?
With fins as polished as gold,
And a dance that you can't stop watching,
Would you stop and stare?

Have you ever seen a dancing shark?
That can dance like a human,
So will you dance with it,
Or will you run for your life?

Tanus Van Molendorff (9)
St Paul's Catholic Primary School, Cheshunt

My Ferocious Lion

When he is tired his eyes go red
Blazing with anger he goes to bed
He likes to dance and sing
He likes to be treated like a king
When he is grumpy he roars
Roar! Roar!
He is a lazy lion
In the day he is cute and kind
But in the night he has another mind
His name is Lollipop
He has a purple top
Lollipop is untamed but clever
He never eats his dinner, never!
He is extraordinary!

Maisie Popely (10)
St Paul's Catholic Primary School, Cheshunt

Angel Bunny

This is my angel bunny
She loves soaring through the air
Making flowers grow
With her magic
But when someone is trying to kill the flowers
She must save them all
She blasts past the trees
Zooms to the sun
Then she lands down
And I wake up
Now I realise she's just made up
I look around my room
It's just pitch-black
No happy, super angel bunny
Just me and my thoughts.

Lottie Leake (10)
St Paul's Catholic Primary School, Cheshunt

Draco The Crazy Ferret

Draco is a ferret,
And a crazy one too,
He is crazy, small and sassy,
His extraordinary fur is so soft,
The way he runs is so peculiar,
His body is so small and delicate,
But he isn't very classy,
He jumps up and down all day,
He never gets tired,
Draco is so mischievous,
His cute little feet pitter-patter on the ground,
He isn't very clever,
But he is tiny, messy and cute.

Evie Toms (10)
St Paul's Catholic Primary School, Cheshunt

Spot The Hilarious Hyena

Spot is a hyena, he roams around all day
Being lazy lying in the shade
He is always hungry and he always complains!
Chomp, chomp, chomp!
As he eats his food using his razor-sharp teeth,
Spot is very friendly,
And is always jumping about,
Boing, boing about,
Even though he is small,
He thinks he is really, really tall,
Spot does nothing all day,
Except play, play, play.

Francesca Smith (10)
St Paul's Catholic Primary School, Cheshunt

The Dog With A Horn

Have you ever seen a dog with a horn?
A dog with a horn, oh yes, a dog with a horn!
And a dog with a horn that neighs every day,
A dog with a horn, oh, a bright rainbow horn.

Have you ever seen a dog with a horn?
A dog with a horn and a short, teeny tail,
And a dog with a horn called Dogocorn!
Oh, a dog with a horn that is a handsome male.

Oh yes, oh yes, oh yes,
A dog with a horn.

Millie O'Sullivan (9)
St Paul's Catholic Primary School, Cheshunt

Moly-Mae The Mouse!

Moly-Mae who thought she was lame,
But her dad tried to tell her she was full of fame,
She was so cute, that meant cameras in her face.

She would always run to her ugly cave,
That had no doors or any hallways,
Her fame would always get in the way.

Dancing would make her feel better,
Moly-Mae was so good at dancing,
Do you have a way of feeling better?
I know I do, what about you?

Imogen Popely (9)
St Paul's Catholic Primary School, Cheshunt

The Ocean Is Never Safe...

Chomp! You are never safe,
I stalk your every move,
Whether you're swimming or diving,
Deep in the big blue ocean,
Lies a dangerous creature waiting to strike,
You're never alone in the ocean,
And you never will be,
Because I will follow you until you get on my nerves,
I stroll through the water at incredible speed,
Waiting for whoever dares to step foot in the ocean...

Lorenzo Guglielmucci (11)
St Paul's Catholic Primary School, Cheshunt

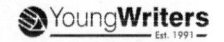

The Peculiar Monkey

Peculiar pet,
It's a colourful thing,
You go to the zoo,
You wouldn't find this pet,
Jumping around as crazy as it could,
With bananas in its hands,
Its colourful body that is pretty eye-catching,
With its friends beside it,
Running away on wooden, brown trees,
They give a gentle laugh,
Can you guess what it is?
A peculiar, colourful monkey.

Ana-Rose Ranasinghe (11)
St Paul's Catholic Primary School, Cheshunt

The Alala Corn Dog

Have you ever seen an Alala Corn Dog?
With wings that flap gloriously and eyes as sparkling as the sun,
They are cute, tiny, clever and lazy,
They like to have fun and be funny,
They like food and water.

Have you ever seen an Alala Corn Dog?
With teeth as blunt as a pencil,
And they like maths and music,
They eat fish and you know they like water.

Brady Pell (9)
St Paul's Catholic Primary School, Cheshunt

Ronny Wonny Is At It Again!

Ronny Wonny is at it again,
He creeps and creeps, gentle and agile,
Cute and sassy and is sure to bring you a smile,
Mischievous and ferocious,
Feathery and simply quite atrocious,
After all, he's only a furry, lazy cat!
He likes to play with colourful mats!
He thinks he's a lion when he is really only a cat,
Ronny Wonny is at it again!

Jalika Jaiteh (11)
St Paul's Catholic Primary School, Cheshunt

Man-Eating Gecko

Have you ever seen the man-eating gecko?
With a tail as hard as rock,
And claws as strong as an angry gorilla,
Would you scream in fear?

Have you ever seen the man-eating gecko?
With eyes as dark as the midnight sky,
And teeth as sharp as a narwhal's horn,
Would you run for your life?

Tell your family.
Save yourself.

Isabelle Aliberti (10)
St Paul's Catholic Primary School, Cheshunt

The Golden Penguin

Golden wings as solid as steel,
He swims to the deep sea and will energise,
When you get close to him,
He will leap out of the water,
He will never bite you, he is very friendly,
Originally, he was a normal penguin,
But one day, he was swimming and drowned,
He met a giant squid,
He would grant him one wish,
And he wished to be golden.

Samuel Robson (9)
St Paul's Catholic Primary School, Cheshunt

The Winged Panda

Have you ever seen a flying panda?
That has two and a half foot long wings,
And fur as fluffy as one thousand fluffy kittens,
Would you trust it to take a ride?

Have you ever seen a flying panda?
With eyes as shiny as a light reflection in a mirror,
And a black nose as black as the sky at midnight,
Would you see it and stare?

Ryan Gibson (9)
St Paul's Catholic Primary School, Cheshunt

The Pop Star Skunk

Have you ever seen a singing skunk?
Hair as blue as a new blue pen,
Eye shadow as bright and shimmery as the sun.
Would you watch or would you run?
Have you ever seen a singing skunk?
With a red guitar like burning flames,
And a cool outfit like ice.
Would you watch the concert?
Go and watch if you like,
Wacky and weird.

Scarlett-Rose Thorogood (9)
St Paul's Catholic Primary School, Cheshunt

The Superhero Puppy

Have you ever seen a superhero puppy?
With a clever brain as big as a colour football,
And eyes as huge as a gigantic pen lid,
Would you faint if you saw this?

The superhero puppy,
Have you ever seen a superhero puppy?
With an adorable, beautiful face,
And a tail as long as a sausage dog,
Would you be surprised?

Nikolai Paton (9)
St Paul's Catholic Primary School, Cheshunt

My Peculiar Pet

My peculiar pet is very clever,
My peculiar pet is adorable when it sleeps,
When it is standing in the sun it is very colourful,
When I hold it in my arms it is gentle,
Can you guess what it is?
It is a monkey!
My favourite animal,
It eats bananas all day long,
It lives in a big cage,
I love my monkey so much!

Poppy Saunders (10)
St Paul's Catholic Primary School, Cheshunt

The Flying Fox!

Have you ever seen a flying fox?
With wings as wide as a goose,
Would you stare or ignore?

Have you ever seen a flying fox?
As cuddly as a cute, furry dog,
Would you stroke or leave?

Have you ever seen a flying fox?
His name is Monggral,
With wings as bright as a shining star,
What will you do?

Ben Hunger (9)
St Paul's Catholic Primary School, Cheshunt

Peculiar Pets

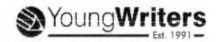

Peculiar pets,
It's a peculiar thing,
We go outside and it's there,
But we do not seem to pay attention,
With cool devices that make them fly,
Cats, they are all smart,
Dogs, they are all funny,
Water, they all drink it,
We all head to see them,
Instead of leaving them out.

Cally de Silva (10)
St Paul's Catholic Primary School, Cheshunt

The Talking Cat

Have you ever seen a talking cat?
With long, white whiskers,
And fur as black as coal,
Would you stop and stare?

Have you ever seen a talking cat?
With some fur as white as snow,
And a voice like the whisper of the wind,
Would you stop and listen to this extraordinary cat?

Isabelle Palmer (9)
St Paul's Catholic Primary School, Cheshunt

The Aiger

Have you ever seen a monster with really spiky hair?
He is intense like a shouting lion,
And never gives up, he keeps on going and going,
And his bond is unbreakable,
And he is agile and clever,
Even incredible, wild and he is an Aiger.

Israel Teniola (9)
St Paul's Catholic Primary School, Cheshunt

Zig And Zog's Adventures

I have two pets,
One called Zig and one called Zog,
They saved the planet once, did you know?
They were on the news!
And laughed at our newts,
'Cause they got jealous,
'Cause they are fiddlywinks,
They always get free drinks,
'Cause they are so rare,
Zig and Zog are very different indeed,
Zig is clever, Zog is not,
And nearly blew the kitchen up!
Bang! Boom! Kaboom! Clunk!
Everything went on the floor,
Next, he drew on the door!
What a mess he made,
Never give Zig your hearing aid,
'Cause he will break it with one big snap!
Now it is the end of the day,
But they want to sleep on hay!

Ava Henry (9)
Whitehouse Primary School, Elm Tree

The Flying Dog!

T he flying dog
H er name is Poppy
E very day I feed her three times a day

F lying around the park, throwing her ball
L ying around, she is tiny but is very loud
Y oung and she is very sassy
I n her room she loves to play
N ever makes any mess any day
G oing on walks is her favourite part of the day

D on't mind her, she is too sassy
O range is one of her favourite colours
G oing to see family, she is very kind.

Olivia Morrison (9)
Whitehouse Primary School, Elm Tree

Space Raiders

My pets are from space
And you're from Earth
Poor Bob and Rob miss Henry, Ellie too
They miss the song Charles sang to them
See Rob in his space bowl
If they see food, they will eat it all
Rob has a space bowl around him
Obnoxiously Rob has to watch Bob eat all of the food
My dog is blue with one little eye
Bob is so gentle and adorable
Peculiar pets indeed
A hamster in a space bowl, you ask?
Come and feel my really soft dog
Don't be scared, they won't bite.

Daniel Wilson (9)
Whitehouse Primary School, Elm Tree

The Picky Punching Pigeon Called Mick

My picky punching pigeon called Mick is very picky,
He likes to punch, but doesn't eat his lunch,
He is a rainbow bird and doesn't speak any words,
He is very small which is very different because I'm very tall,
My picky punching pigeon called Mick has friends,
One called Bob, he is a parrot and one called Gary,
My pet wears boxing gloves that he loves,
The only thing he likes to eat are sticks which he picks.

Scarlett Lowe (10)
Whitehouse Primary School, Elm Tree

Dangerous Dino Dan

My dinosaur called Dan,
Loves to eat an apple flan!
He appeared at my door and I invited him in,
But then he went and ate the peach in a tin!
He ran around the house crushing everything in his path,
And he ended up having a bath!
I told him to sleep in the shed,
But then he went to sleep in my bed!
I woke up in the morning and guess what I did see,
I looked into the garden and saw my apple tree - empty!

Stanley McDougall (10)
Whitehouse Primary School, Elm Tree

The Lazy Dog That Lives In Space!

S he or he loves to live in space
P assing through planets
A nd being as bright as the sun
C hecking if meteorites hit the great places of Earth
E ating meteorites as its food every day

D odging moon earthquakes as they set
O beying lovely space with his or her friends the aliens
G uarding and digging lovely space.

Lincoln Turner (10)
Whitehouse Primary School, Elm Tree

Lazy Lizard

L azy lizard is so lazy
A rrived in my house
Z ara went straight on the sofa
Y es, I am back here, woo!

L azy lizard is fast
I t's even faster than you think
Z ana was also green and white
A nd he was living in a hot country
R ound 140C degrees
D efinitely a very scaly lizard.

Alyssia Whalsh (9)
Whitehouse Primary School, Elm Tree

The Sleeping Dragon

He sleeps in the mornings,
And he comes out at night,
He lives in the trees,
We have to take him out to eat,
He's really obsessed with trees,
He's scared of birds,
He's still a baby,
He likes to whistle like a bird,
He gets really muddy when he's in the mud,
He's really pretty when he reflects the stars,
And really fun.

Rubin Vallily (9)
Whitehouse Primary School, Elm Tree

Super Snail Bob

S uper snail Bob is so long
U nder a shell where he belongs
P lease don't race, I am fast
E veryone else will end up last
R un, run, run

S uper snail Bob, I love you
N ever race me again
A ll the time I'll always be first
I will win all races
L ove racing I do.

Jack Devine (9)
Whitehouse Primary School, Elm Tree

The Tortoise Who Flies

T he tortoise who likes to fly
O riginal animal who likes pies
R apid Bob who likes to run
T ortoise who also likes fun
O bviously Bob likes cats
I like him sitting on mats (instead of mud)
S uperpowered Bob flies everywhere
E ven though he eats a lot, he won't go over there.

Katie Kingston (9)
Whitehouse Primary School, Elm Tree

Dangerous, Wild Kangaroo

When I walked over the bridge,
I saw a black kangaroo,
And it was running in circles,
It looked wild like a pile of dirt,
It was jumping and hopping around like a bunny,
It had scales with black and brown fur,
So it was going to be warm all the time,
And it's like a campfire,
Then it ran as fast as the rainbow.

Rhys Pink (9)
Whitehouse Primary School, Elm Tree

Long Dog

L ong as a giraffe's neck
O n the long dog you can fit five children
N o adult can believe how long he is
G o, go, he is as quick as a gazelle

D on't give him a bone or he will go hyper
O h, at the end of the day he sleeps till 5am
G o catch him if you can.

Christine Petrik (9)
Whitehouse Primary School, Elm Tree

The Ferocious Lemon And Lime Alien Frog

The scary, alien frog is a dangerous, ferocious, lemon and lime tasting alien frog.
It has wings as tiny as a bunch of ants,
One more thing about the ferocious alien frog,
Its incredible body and wings are just like lemon and lime,
With a ferocious, dangerous bite.

Guy Honeyman (9)
Whitehouse Primary School, Elm Tree

Dave The Dumb Tortoise

The tortoise goes to Japan
Looking like a Frenchman
The tortoise poisons the mayor
Which will be a new major
The tortoise goes to Hell
Even though he is putting on hair gel
The tortoise realises he's dead
Even though he's in bed in his head.

Finlay Tombling (9)
Whitehouse Primary School, Elm Tree

The Meerkat Mouse

The meerkat mouse is a meerkat that acts like a mouse,
This is a very fast meerkat, the fastest in the world,
This meerkat loves cheese,
This is certainly the rarest mouse in the world,
The meerkat is very small,
This meerkat is very lazy sometimes.

Mo Khalid (9)
Whitehouse Primary School, Elm Tree

The Weird, Strange Turtle

T he weird, strange turtle is called Billy
U nicorns are what Billy eats
R un if you see him, he might eat your feet
T im is his best friend
L egs for dessert
E lves are what he hates, so elves you better run!

Aleah McGarvey (9)
Whitehouse Primary School, Elm Tree

The Tiny Tiger

T igers love to eat leaves
I gloos are what they live in
G rass is the thing that they play on
E ggs are what tigers hate
R ound the igloos is loads of ice and grass.

Chyna-Rose Whitton (9)
Whitehouse Primary School, Elm Tree

Fire

F ire the name of my alligator
I t is scared of the water
R emember, it is a snake and it is an alligator
E mbrace with my pet alligator.

Daiton Lewis (9)
Whitehouse Primary School, Elm Tree